SOMEDAY, MAYBE, FOREVER

Verses from the Heart

SHIRLEY SIATON

SOMEDAY, MAYBE, FOREVER
Verses from the Heart

Copyright © 2024 Shirley Siaton Parabia

ALL RIGHTS RESERVED.

No part of this book may be reproduced or used in any manner without the prior written permission of the copyright owner, except for the use of brief quotations in a book review. To request permission, contact the publisher at books@inkysword.com.

ISBN 978-621-8371-50-7 (hardcover)

Published by Shirley S. Parabia
Interior formatting by MSM Drive
Cover design by Covers by Sophie

First Edition, October 2024

Inky Sword Book Publishing
Barangay Quezon, Arevalo, Iloilo City 5000
Republic of the Philippines
inkysword.com

SOMEDAY, MAYBE, FOREVER

Verses from the Heart

CONTENTS

Verses from the Heart

Someday

First Taste	21
Living	25
Graduation Day	29
Dumbstruck	35
My Death Man	39
Other	43

Maybe

Afar	53
Arms	57
Away	61
Deception	65
Despair	69
Untold	73

Forever

Aimless	83
Anchor	87
Ardor	91
Depths	95
Desire	99

VERSES FROM THE HEART

On 20th April 2023, I released a compilation of love poems, 'Beloved,' in honor of what would have been my parents' 43rd wedding anniversary. This was a limited release book, meant as a gift to my mother.

Later that year, I decided to expand the poetry collection with a few real-life letters, salvaged from the darkest, deepest corners of my heart and computer hard drives.

Thus, 'Someday, Maybe, Forever: Verses from the Heart' (October 2023), came into being, for release to a wider audience.

The pieces in this book were penned since high school up until adulthood. I would like to believe there are so many aspects, phases and stages of love captured within these pages.

Let us revisit those profound feelings that come with crushes, infatuation and passion. These are the experiences – sweet, bitter or broken - that made us what we are, today.

Here are slices of my heart, dear reader: little bits of someday, maybe and forever.

SOMEDAY

SOMEDAY, MAYBE, FOREVER
VERSES FROM THE HEART

I have not spoken to you for a long time. I suppose we will never speak again.

I don't know how we drifted apart. Perhaps, along the way, amidst the pain we had to endure, we had forgotten ourselves.

I just want you to know that I am sorry, so very sorry, for everything I have not done.

For not being there for you when you needed someone, for not being there when you were hurt and wanting and nobody wanted you around. For not being there when you felt empty and cold and alone.

I just want to let you know that I loved you. Maybe that is all there is to it.

I loved you. The very moment I laid eyes on you, I knew that you were the one I have been waiting for.

I remember you were sitting, and looking down at a piece of paper, and you were squinting like you could barely see. You were absorbed in that simple moment, of seeking something, that I loved you and wished that maybe someday you will try to find me the same way you tried to look for something written on that paper.

You did find me. You found me, and did not let go ever since.

SHIRLEY SIATON

I tried to forget you. I tried to love so many others, yet they all failed in my eyes. Because they were not you. No one will ever be you.

No one will ever look at me that same way you did. I saw something greater in myself when you looked at me, that all was possible and I could endure all the pain thrown at me. That nothing was unbearable, and that there was always tomorrow.

Maybe, in some other time, we will see each other again. Maybe, someday, nothing will come between us. Maybe, someday, we will not both hurt as we had before.

I wish I could hold you one last time and tell you that I will always be there in my own way. All you need ever do is find me again.

Then, maybe, we shall have our chance.

Someday.

SOMEDAY, MAYBE, FOREVER
VERSES FROM THE HEART

FIRST TASTE

Pounding.

The weary floor resonates:
infectious with life and sound,
with strobes of varicolored light.
In flashes.
As fast as the young heart
pumps life,
as sharp as the senses
take in the reek of body heat.

My bareness
is shaped by your hands;
I move to the rhythm
shared by lone strangers
amidst the frenzy.
I forget the bitch wind
of night.

This is but the first touch.

SHIRLEY SIATON

As the swirling
gathers me into its billows,
I hold on to flesh, bone,
the unmasked scent of soap
and the unmistakable froth of anger
bubbling from burnished lips
and distinctly hear

The pounding.

SOMEDAY, MAYBE, FOREVER
VERSES FROM THE HEART

LIVING

I live this strange little
existence—I don't even know
what it's supposed to be.
Strangled, laden with
shattered stuff:
fragments of a heart once beating
and pumping tangy blood.

I breathe this so-called air of life
that kills me with each
proverbial toke—
when I would have wanted the
glamor of cigarette smoke.

I roam the cruel streets
that scream of my
generation's apathy.
And bleed with red and sunny-yellow
and acetylene-white.
Words, their wisdom
long lost.

SHIRLEY SIATON

> I love this wisp
> of a being ready
> to be snapped in two.
> He's the one who
> means so much;
> enough that I just have to
> go on.
> Living.

SOMEDAY, MAYBE, FOREVER
VERSES FROM THE HEART

GRADUATION DAY

It dawns like a day
Of impending doom:
I stand on the cracked second-floor corridor
And stare at the rusty bars
Of the three-decade-old balcony.

A guttural prayer escapes
my chapped lips
For I forgot the balm
(forgot to shoplift)
So I bite my dry lower lip
In supplication to a higher power.

My uniform is worn down,
The collar is blackish-brown;
Mama forgot to wash it (again):
The mahjong table takes up
Her laundry hours.

A footfall draws me to reality.
It was him:

SHIRLEY SIATON

A lanky boy of burnt-red skin
And a voice that sometimes squeaks
When he shouts to be fed
During basketball.

Dressed in scuffed brown-leather shoes
And a half-open shirtjack,
He reeks of a citrusy scent
That costs sixty-five pesos
A bottle.

He stops by my monobloc
And asks if he could copy our last assignment:
Ten multi-colored graphs in Calculus;
I say no
(I don't know why).

He shrugs and, whistling, walks away
Like everybody had in my
Four years spent in a
Tomb of things
I'd want to forget.

SOMEDAY, MAYBE, FOREVER
VERSES FROM THE HEART

(And so
The toga tassel is turned
From back-left
to front right)

Yet will always remember.

SOMEDAY, MAYBE, FOREVER
VERSES FROM THE HEART

DUMBSTRUCK

Now is not the time
To tell me that you're sorry
Just go on and don't look back
That's what I expect you to do

There is so much to say
Too many words rooted
In the depths of your eyes
You just can't put them to words

I've never said much, have I?
I'm mute as a mime when I'm near you
Then again, there's not much to say
For now, you're on your way

Don't say a word
Don't even look my way
Don't dare say you're sorry
Though I doubt I'll make it through another day
Without you

SHIRLEY SIATON

I have not said I love you
And now I've lost the chance to
Say goodbye
Allow me one final embrace
That I will feel
Forever

SOMEDAY, MAYBE, FOREVER
VERSES FROM THE HEART

MY DEATH MAN

lightning strikes you
and you stand ramrod
straight
silver bullets pounce
on your obsidian heart
and you stand
impervious

what's your name,
my death man?
who are you
to take my breath
away
and leave me
seeking?
my death man,
come to me
relieve me of misery

the acid shower
caresses
your unyielding face

SHIRLEY SIATON

that I yearn to caress—
the downpour is reduced
to the trickles
of music
from your splintered guitar

daggers of desolation
draw your black-red blood
and my lips savor
its metal tang
then I drink
of your madness
and the coldness
of your love

my death man,
your music is my eternal lullaby
my death man,
your music is my elegy

SOMEDAY, MAYBE, FOREVER
VERSES FROM THE HEART

OTHER

I was the one
Who looked at you from way
across the room
The one who felt your pain
And never gave it back
I cared not
If you can't even see
Just in dreams
Be with me

I was the girl
Who felt your touch
On her flesh
That gentleness from someone so strong
I cried not
If you love her
Just go on
Walking past

SHIRLEY SIATON

I was the other
You looked right through
I was part of you
That shudder in the hall
That whisper into the moonless sky
That gaze on your back as you walk towards her
That one
Loving you

MAYBE

SOMEDAY, MAYBE, FOREVER
VERSES FROM THE HEART

My love for him shall live in the deepest shadows, in the darkest recesses of my heart.

So many years ago, moments so short, so stolen, they should have been long forgotten. These are moments I will never forget until the day I die.

For he was the only man who cared enough to wish that I find my true destiny. He touched me so gently, and embraced me, and kissed me. And then I never saw him again.

Years have gone by since I saw him last. I could never confide in anyone as I have confided in him. I could never tell anybody else the madness that I told him. The madness that he understood and never judged.

Perhaps, in another life, in another time, I will see him again. Maybe then I will get to thank him once more, for saving my life.

He gave me a reason to go on living, this man. He made me feel that I wasn't alone, that I will never be alone, because, somehow, he will always be with me.

He was the only man who loved me the way I always have been – flimsy, delicate, broken.

The only one who cared enough to put together pieces of me, only to tear it all apart with goodbye.

SOMEDAY, MAYBE, FOREVER
VERSES FROM THE HEART

AFAR

You are so far above
There is no road for me to take
To touch you, or reach for you
But I would leave all I have
For your sake

You are flawed and human
Yet they embrace all that you are
The way I would take you in my arms, too
But I never could
Because you are so far

I may never hold you close
You may never be mine
The way I want it to be
But my heart is yours
Until the end of time

From afar
I will look at you
From a distance
I will be there for you
From the shadows
I will give you all my love

SHIRLEY SIATON

If only I could have a moment
I would stop time
To be with you
If only I could live in dreams
Then I would fly to you

All these could never be
Yet I won't stop loving you

SOMEDAY, MAYBE, FOREVER
VERSES FROM THE HEART

ARMS

Living in the stony silence of night
In the dark embrace of solitude
Listening to the echoes
In the empty halls of your heart–
Songs evil, lost, divine.

Through it all, though consumed,
Half-rotted by pride;
What your heart shall say
That I will abide.

I love you
Though you are still in pain
(from what had been)
How can I break through these walls
To hold you in my arms again?

SOMEDAY, MAYBE, FOREVER
VERSES FROM THE HEART

AWAY

Remember my tears
They were shed for the loneliness
That I saw in your eyes
I tried to end the pain
But my own weakness wounds me

Remember my laughter
It rang because of hope
That each new day brings
I held on to the light
But darkness always comes

Remember my words
I write them for forever
I tried to make memories endure
But time washes away
These fleeting dreams made of sand

Remember my heart
It has always been yours
My love has never faded, only flourished
I tried to tell you
But I cannot always speak

SHIRLEY SIATON

I love you
Please remember this

DECEPTION

Just don't listen to me
I lie
Time and time again
Until the falsehoods
Fall from my lips
As easily as breathing

Just don't say a word
I won't heed you
As always
You ask for nothing
You give everything
Without doubt

Just don't come any closer
I will push you away
With every moment
I am weaker
I am afraid
I can no longer hide

SHIRLEY SIATON

Just don't look at me
I can't bear the promise in your eyes
That you will fight for me
Without question
When asked to
But we are not just meant to be

Just walk away
Before I hold you back
Just leave
Before I run towards you
Just forget me
Before I learn to love you
Even more

Just stop

SOMEDAY, MAYBE, FOREVER
VERSES FROM THE HEART

DESPAIR

Believe me
When I tell you that
I see hope in your eyes
Believe me
When I tell you that
I see strength in your pain
And my salvation in your
carefully concealed despair

Believe me
When I look into your eyes
And say I see tears unshed
Believe me
When I try to touch your soul
But never could
And the cold simply
rips my heart apart

Believe me
When I say goodbye
In a halting whisper
Believe me
When I turn away
From your compelling madness

SHIRLEY SIATON

Believe me
That I am sorry
for being with you
That I love what I can
never have
That I walk away from you
before I no longer could

Believe me

SOMEDAY, MAYBE, FOREVER
VERSES FROM THE HEART

UNTOLD

You said that you were sorry
That you don't need me anymore
You said that you were leaving
And walked right out the door

How many times have you hurt me?
I truly have stopped counting
How many times have you left me?
Standing alone while it was raining

You said that all was wrong
That nothing works when we're together
You said we would only be lying
If we keep talking of forever

So go on, tell me
Whatever you want to say
Go on, be true
There seems to be no other way

SHIRLEY SIATON

Tell me I'm not the ideal
I know all your reasons why
Tell me I'll never be strong
That I'm always lacking in your eyes

Tell me everything that hurts
This forever hopeful heart of mine
Tell me how to make you stay
Just don't tell me goodbye

FOREVER

SOMEDAY, MAYBE, FOREVER
VERSES FROM THE HEART

You came into my life when I most needed you in it.

I was running away and nursing my wounds like a battered animal, with every intention of hiding in the embrace of darkness, unseen and unheard.

When I saw you that fateful evening, I knew in my heart of hearts that you would be the one to bring me back to life, back into the light.

You are an angel rising from the ashes of my razed hopes. You are everything I have ever really needed: someone pure and true, someone strong and unselfish and so beautiful of soul.

You gave me the kind of love that I needed, the kind of life I was meant for, a precious and dazzling happiness so few will ever know.

We have weathered so many storms and grown up so much since the beginning.

No matter what happens, I will be here next to you, holding your hand and kissing your perpetually furrowed brow, giving you as much love and care as I could, without limits and conditions.

For what you have given, since the beginning, is without measure and could never be matched in this life or the next.

I love you, now and forever and after.

AIMLESS

Shall I wait for you?
I scorn and shun
The moments when you are not by my side
You wander aimlessly
Reticent and seeking

Shall I look into your eyes?
I fear and dread
The time when I could no longer lie
I pretend uselessly
My will is futile and bent

Shall I touch you?
I do not wish to
Because the moment I do
You will know the truth
That I hide

Shall I speak to you?
My words come listlessly
Hiding my true yearning
I shall say
The things I do not mean

SHIRLEY SIATON

Shall I love you?
My heart could never lie
Even if forever I persist
To deceive it, and deny
That it has long since belonged to you

I have to try

SOMEDAY, MAYBE, FOREVER
VERSES FROM THE HEART

ANCHOR

Call for my passion
Heedless as I am
Reckless and unstoppable
I shall hear you
Sadness and hate
May consume me
But never
Shall I turn away
From you

Speak to my soul
As I wait for hope
Being the child
That I always will be
Love shall be my anchor
In this stormy sea
Lighting my path of uncertainty
As forever
I believe it shall endure
Give your heart
To me

SOMEDAY, MAYBE, FOREVER
VERSES FROM THE HEART

ARDOR

I wish that we may be together
In a way that we fear nothing
And believe in everything
That we have

I wish that we may be stronger
In a way that we do not hold back tears
But cry freely to let the pain out
So what's left inside is happiness
And hope, perhaps

I wish that we may love as purely
As the spring rushes over the rocks
That the years will wear our bodies away
But our hearts never stop flowing
Towards eternity

SOMEDAY, MAYBE, FOREVER
VERSES FROM THE HEART

DEPTHS

You have nothing, you say
Nothing to fight for
No reason to live or die
No battle, nor twisted reasons to lie
Just an empty heart beating
Deep into the moonless night

You have everything, you say
Everything to hate and shun
Pained endlessly
In the merciless light of the sun
All the countless whispers
Of judgment and persecution
Everything to carry, burdened evermore
Deep into your loneliness

You have me, you say
I to fight against, or madly hate
To die with, perhaps
To share your pain
In the harsh embrace of a cruel life
I gather the fragments
Of a heart long since unfound
And try so hard
To make you whole once more

SHIRLEY SIATON

And I have you, I say
To hold on to, to madly love
To live with—forever, perhaps
Or maybe beyond

In this unyielding existence
We shall find ourselves once more
So give me your heart
And we'll have our love to fight for

SOMEDAY, MAYBE, FOREVER
VERSES FROM THE HEART

DESIRE

I feel my heart steaming towards you
I am wrought with the flames
Of passion
Consuming me
Until I am nothing more
Than smoldering ash

I feel my body steaming towards you
I am drawn without resistance
To your fiery seduction
Burning deep into me
Until I am nothing more
Than trembling desire

I feel my mind steaming towards you
I am controlled by this irresistible fascination
And unrelenting obsession
Taking over me
Until I am nothing more
Than sheer madness

SHIRLEY SIATON

I feel my soul steaming towards you
I shall sweetly surrender
All that I have
And all that make me
Until I am nothing more
Than your wasted possession

ABOUT THE AUTHOR

Shirley Siaton writes edgy and evocative poems and stories. Her worlds are in a deliciously dark cross-section of the romance, neo-noir, action, fantasy, new adult and contemporary genres.

She has several books of poetry and fiction released since February 2023. Her first book is the free verse collection *'Black Cat and other poems.'* She also pens juvenile literature as Shirley Parabia.

She is an award-winning writer, poet and journalist in English, Filipino and Hiligaynon, lauded by the Stevan Javellana Foundation, Philippine Information Agency and West Visayas State University. Her essays, short stories and poems have been published internationally in print and digital media. Her multi-lingual plays have been staged in the Philippines.

Shirley is a black belt in Shotokan Karate and an international certified fitness coach. Originally from Iloilo City, she is based in the Middle East with her husband and two daughters.

LINKS

Shirley's official website:
shirleysiaton.com

Complete reading guide:
shirley.pub

Subscribe to Shirley's VIP list for free exclusive updates:
newsletter.shirleysiaton.com

www.ingramcontent.com/pod-product-compliance
Lightning Source LLC
LaVergne TN
LVHW092009090526
838202LV00002B/59